Introduction 5

Question 1 7
I think I'm a Christian, but I'm not sure. How can I be certain?

Question 2 10
How could God possibly forgive what I've done?

Question 3 14
I get so distracted when I try to read the Bible. How can I focus?

Question 4 21
My prayer life feels weak. How can I pray more effectively?

Question 5 26
Do I really need the Church?

Question 6 31
If God loves me, why am I suffering?

Question 7 35
I'm struggling to forgive people who have wronged me. Can you help?

Question 8 40
I'm confused about the gender debate. What does the Bible say?

Question 9 45
What is revival? Can we really experience it?

Question 10 50
Can Christians really make a difference?

Small Group Guide 54

Notes 66

Introduction

While you might go to Google to ask how long to cook your fourteen-pound Thanksgiving turkey, for your most important questions you want to go to a source you know you can trust.

That's why the team at *Revive Our Hearts* receives lots of questions from listeners with searching hearts. It's also why we've decided to bring answers to some of our most frequently asked questions directly to you. The purpose of this booklet is not to give you comprehensive answers. Instead, we hope to give you handles to hold on to as you wrestle with these essential questions.

This booklet is also designed to be used as a tool in group settings. Gather with your small group or Sunday school class and work through these essential questions together. Reach out to a friend or neighbor who might be new to following Christ, and use these questions to jump-start meaningful conversations about faith. We've included a small group guide in the back of the booklet to help.

Throughout this resource you'll find "Seeking Answers from Scripture" sections containing a few verses to get you started. Believing that God's Word is the ultimate answer book, we'd encourage you to open your Bible and dig into these verses for yourself. You'll find a more extensive list of Scriptures along with recommended resources in the small group guide.

Ask away! And be sure to visit our website at ReviveOurHearts.com for more answers grounded in God's Word.

Question 1

I think I'm a Christian, but I'm not sure. How can I be certain?

A: While the Bible is a book containing many answers, it is also a book that raises many questions. Many people, including people of great faith, have asked probing questions about God and the way He calls us to live.

Consider Nicodemus, a religious leader whose questions are recorded in John 3. Perhaps he thought he knew the answers to essential questions about life and faith. But did he have the right answers? Did he even ask the right questions? John 3:1–21 describes Nicodemus coming to Jesus under the cover of night. Their conversation confronts us with a very important question: Who do we think Jesus is? And are we sure our answer is right? Nicodemus thought he knew, but he was wrong.

READ JOHN 3:1–21 AND WRITE DOWN THE QUESTIONS NICODEMUS ASKED JESUS.

_____

_____

_____

Nicodemus asked an essential question we all must settle: Who are you, Jesus? If Jesus was just a good teacher, we can take what we like from His words and ignore the rest. If He was simply a prophet, we can respect His wisdom in the same way we might respect other historical figures. But if He is Lord as He claimed, we must respond by surrendering to His authority in our lives.

Jesus' response to Nicodemus' question was this: "Truly, truly, I say to you, unless one is born again he cannot see the kingdom of God" (v. 3).

Jesus was describing the spiritual rebirth that happens when someone yields his or her life to Jesus and becomes a Christian. This concept was mysterious to Nicodemus, and it can feel mysterious to us. We wonder: Am I really a Christian? How can I know if I have been born again? How can I be sure that I have been saved from sin and death and have confidence in my eternal life?

Nicodemus asked similar questions: "How can these things be?" (v. 9).

The answer Jesus gave is one of the most beloved and powerful statements in all of Scripture: "For God so loved the world, that he gave his only Son, that whoever believes in him should not perish but have eternal life" (v. 16).

Jesus did the most important work of salvation through His death on the cross. A person becomes a Christian when he or she believes that Jesus is who He said He is and responds in faith. Jesus also explained the powerful result of this decision—we move from death to life. Instead of perishing as a result of our sin, we have the promise of spending eternity alive with Jesus. He saves us!

GRACE THROUGH FAITH

Your eternal destiny is not determined by the life that you have lived, the sins you have committed, the good works you have done—or by how much theology you know. You can have confidence that you are a follower of Christ if you have put your faith in Jesus, believing that on the cross He took the punishment and hell you deserved for your sins and gave you His righteousness and the promise of heaven in exchange. This is the good news of the gospel.

The apostle Paul summed it up this way: "For by grace you have been saved through faith. And this is not your own doing; it is the gift of God" (Eph. 2:8).

Grace is a gift, given to you by Jesus when you put your faith in Him. **The essential question, therefore, is not what *you* have done, but rather, whether you have believed and received what *He* has done for you.**

If you haven't, repent and believe. Christ died for you so that you could be reconciled to God. If you have, you can know that you are indeed a Christian and that He has adopted you into His family. Even when questions or doubts arise, you can rest in this promise, "I give them eternal life, and they will never perish, and no one will snatch them out of my hand. My Father, who has given them to me, is greater than all, and no one is able to snatch them out of the Father's hand" (John 10:28–29).

God's hands are bigger than your wavering faith. Your salvation is not going to be lost. It will be kept—by God, your Keeper.

SEEKING ANSWERS FROM GOD'S WORD

- 1 Corinthians 15:1–11
- Ephesians 2:1–10
- Titus 2:11–14

Question 2

How could God possibly forgive what I've done?

A: "Where to begin?"

That is the question Krista started with when she wrote to *Revive Our Hearts*.

Krista carried the heavy weights of sin and guilt for many years.

> My last years of high school I participated in sexual acts, telling myself that it was okay because I never actually "went all the way," but in my heart I knew it was wrong. I would go home and literally wash myself raw in the shower. I wanted to wash away the shame of my own sin, because I didn't understand Jesus had already done it for me!

In Krista's letter, she shared that she started drinking with friends and sleeping with her boyfriend. She got pregnant unexpectedly and seriously considered abortion. Though she eventually decided to keep the baby and she and her boyfriend got married, she continued to struggle. Krista was bitter toward her husband, disillusioned with her faith, and ready for a divorce.

The weight of past sins (or current realities) can feel incredibly burdensome. Like Krista, you might live with guilt over past sexual sin. Maybe you also faced an unplanned pregnancy but made a different choice and now live with haunting guilt. Maybe you carry the shame of a failed relationship, an unwise financial decision, or a different pattern of sin. Perhaps a temptation pulls at you so strongly that you fear you'll never overcome it. You may doubt that God's grace can cover your repeated failures.

A HEAVY DEBT

We sin when we neglect to do what God says we must do or when we do what God says we must not do. We also sin when we do right things with the wrong heart, when we want the wrong things in life, or when we love something more than God. Because God is holy, He cannot tolerate our sin. Our sin separates us from Him. This separation can make the weight of our sin feel unbearably heavy.

Since "all have sinned and fall short of the glory of God" (Rom. 3:23), we all need a way to be reconciled to God. Because God loves us (John 3:16), He delights to extend mercy toward us (Heb. 4:16), but because God is just, He cannot simply ignore or dismiss our sin.

Romans 6:23 reveals that sin is costly: "For the wages of sin is death."

The debt of our sin must be paid. God could have insisted we make the payment ourselves, and He would have been just in doing so. Instead, He sent to earth His holy Son Jesus, who had no debt of His own, to assume our debt and through His death pay the penalty required.

Our debt—all that we owed—was transferred to Jesus Christ when He gave His life on the cross.

Second Corinthians 5:21 declares, "For our sake he made him to be sin who knew no sin, so that in him we might become the righteousness of God."

Those who trust in Jesus—not in themselves, in their religious works, in their efforts, in their penance, or in their good deeds, but in Christ as their guilt-bearer and substitute—are pronounced debt-free before a holy God.

Christ's sacrifice at Calvary is sufficient to forgive every sin that has ever been committed—even yours. He has purchased forgiveness for you, and He offers it to you as a gift.

If your own sin feels unforgivable, consider: are you resting in God's power and promise to forgive, or are you trying to earn God's mercy in your own strength?

It takes faith to say, "I cannot earn God's forgiveness. I will accept what Christ has done as sufficient payment for my sin." If you're feeling squashed by the weight of your sin, ask God to give you the faith to believe that He has already done everything required to cancel its burden.

BRING SIN INTO THE LIGHT

Though you cannot earn forgiveness, God's Word calls you to repent and to be honest with God, willingly acknowledging your sin and asking for grace.

> If we confess our sins, he is faithful and just to forgive us our sins and to cleanse us from all unrighteousness. (1 John 1:9)

Instead of simply asking God to help you be a better person, repentance requires agreeing with Him on the seriousness of your sin and confessing it when you have rebelled against Him.

Scripture also encourages Christ's followers to confess our sins to other Christ-followers so that we can hold each other accountable and drag what is hidden into the light (James 5:16).

When Krista accepted Christ's forgiveness, even for the sins that most haunted her, she experienced true freedom.

> To look back at where I was—just wow, God! He delivered me away from abortion, divorce, hurt and broken relationships, and a life of feeling inadequate and shameful to a life of healing and never needing to measure up, because Christ took all of my shame and all of my sin on Himself because He loves me. God loves me! That's all I need! I don't look for my joy and fulfillment in people anymore. Only God. Through Christ's work, God is the only thing that will ever give me true peace, joy, and fulfillment.

Jesus paid a tremendous price so that your sins could be forgiven. The cross is big enough to carry even your most grievous sins. You could never earn this gift, but you can respond by repenting of your sin, asking God to help you turn toward righteousness, and praising Him for His mercy toward you.

SEEKING ANSWERS FROM GOD'S WORD

- Isaiah 1:18
- Acts 3:18–21
- Ephesians 1:7–8

Question 3

I get so distracted when I try to read the Bible. How can I focus?

A: In an era of quick sound bites and social media posts, it can be challenging to focus on anything of length, much less commit to reading the Bible, a book made up of sixty-six smaller books, written over the course of 1,500 years, by more than forty human authors. Yet knowing the Bible is essential to spiritual growth.

As *Revive Our Hearts* founder Nancy DeMoss Wolgemuth says,

> Your relationship with God will never be any greater than your relationship with His Word. You cannot claim to know God if you don't know God's Word. You can't claim to love God if you don't love God's Word. You can't claim to obey God if you don't obey God's Word.[1]

You don't need to have a seminary degree in order to study the Bible. Understanding God's Word is attainable for every believer through the power of the Holy Spirit. But where do you start? A desire to study the Bible is evidence of His work in your heart, but what can you do when you struggle to read God's Word consistently or when focusing on God's Word becomes a frequent challenge?

KEEP THE MAIN THING THE MAIN THING

Before you reach for a new Bible study or download a fresh Bible reading plan to jump-start your study of the Word, pause and consider your motivations. While the Bible is a mirror that helps us rightly see ourselves and while it does give practical wisdom for how to live our daily lives, the Bible is not primarily a book about us. The Bible is a book about God. The purpose of the Scriptures is to reveal who God is.

Consider your objectives when you open your Bible:

- Is your primary goal to know God's character?

- Is God's Word the lens through which you see the world or is the world the lens through which you see the Bible?

- Do you primarily go to the Bible for comfort and inspiration?

- When you read your Bible, what kinds of questions do you ask of the text?

If your primary objective in Bible study is to learn more about yourself, you will struggle to engage with Scripture. There are simply too many other means by which you can focus on yourself. But when we open God's Word looking to find more of Him, we will find that our desire to know Him through His Word will only grow.

FILL UP YOUR TOOL BOX

There is likely a place in your home where you keep a few tools. Perhaps a drawer contains a hammer and a set of screwdrivers or a toolbox in your garage contains wrenches, zip ties, and a paint brush or two. Common problems occur in every home. It's important to know where your flat head screwdriver is when you need to replace an outlet cover or where your paintbrush is when you need to touch up the trim.

In the same way, it is wise to have access to a set of tools as you study God's Word. Then when common problems like inability to focus, waning passion, and lack of comprehension arise, you'll be ready.

Here are some tools we recommend.

STUDY BY TOPIC

Spend time seeking the Lord through prayer about an area of spiritual growth you wish to pursue. Then take the following steps:

- Humbly approach the topic of study, recognizing that although you may have some knowledge there is still much to learn and apply to your life.

- Study several Scriptures pertaining to the particular topic using a concordance. Look up a few references at a time, jotting down your observations and questions as you go and cross-referencing related passages.

- Record passages that are particularly meaningful or thought-provoking on index cards or in a journal. Use them for memorization and further meditation.

- Research and borrow or purchase trusted books on the particular topic, including commentaries. Use resources as you would a school textbook. Don't just casually read, but thoroughly study the subject.

- Be inquisitive. Ask questions as you read Scripture, as you are in conversation with others, and as you go through your day in prayer.

- Share with others what God is teaching you. Allow your transparency and need for wisdom in this area to be an inspiration for others to follow in pursuing spiritual maturity.

STUDY A WHOLE PASSAGE OR BOOK OF THE BIBLE

To study an entire section of Scripture, try the inductive Bible study method. This method involves answering three questions:

1. What does this say? (Observation)
2. What does this mean? (Interpretation)
3. What should I do? (Application)

TIPS FOR MAKING OBSERVATIONS

- **Summarize:** After reading a passage, try to come up with a title. Look for a key verse that captures the heart of the passage. Write a brief summary of the passage, including the major points.

- **Paraphrase**: Try to write the passage in your own words.

- **Ask questions:**
  - Who wrote this? About whom? Speaking to whom?
  - What happened? What are the main events? The major themes?

- When was this written?
- Where did this happen?
- Why was this written?

- **Look for patterns:** Repeated words or phrases can help you understand what the author intends to emphasize.
- **Look for cross-references:** As you become more familiar with the Bible, you'll find that as you read a passage, the Holy Spirit will bring to mind other verses that relate to, confirm, or shed further light on what you're reading.

TIPS FOR INTERPRETATION

Ask these kinds of questions to help you understand the implications of the text.

- What does this passage teach me about God?
- What does this passage teach me about the gospel?
- What does this passage teach me about man?
- Are there any promises to hold on to?
- Are there any commands to obey?
- Are there any examples to follow?
- Are there any sins to avoid?

TIPS FOR APPLICATION

After you've learned the "what," ask the question, "So what?" with questions like these:

- In view of this Truth, what changes need to be made in my life?

- What practical steps can I take to apply this Truth to my life?

THE A-E-I-O-U BIBLE STUDY METHOD

Whether studying by topic or by section, another method you can apply to your study is the A-E-I-O-U Method.

"A"—Ask questions

As you're reading the Word of God, ask questions like these:

- Who wrote this book?
- When was this written?
- What does this passage say?
- What are the major events?
- When did these events take place?
- Where did this happen?
- What are the main ideas?
- Why was this written?
- What does this passage mean?

"E"—Emphasize key words and phrases

Look for a key verse in the chapter that captures the heart of the passage. Search for key words, patterns, repeated words or phrases, and things that recur in the passage, chapter, or book. Then summarize what the book teaches about those subjects.

"I"—In your own words

Write a brief summary or an overview of the passage in your own words. What is this about? Include the major points. This helps in meditating on and thinking about the passage.

"O"—Other related Scriptures

Look for other related Scriptures, or cross-references. There are two tools that will help. One is an exhaustive concordance, which lists every word found in the Bible. Under each of those words is a list of every place where that word appears in Scripture. As you pull these verses together, you'll find that they interconnect.

Another tool is called *The Treasury of Scripture Knowledge*. This tool goes through the Bible and next to each verse gives other references that align with the theme of that verse.

"U"—Use it in application

Everything we read in God's Word calls for some sort of response. It may be to exercise faith in God's promises or His character, to humble ourselves, to acknowledge our need, to confess a sin, or to turn from a wrong way of thinking. It may be to worship and adore the God who has revealed Himself in Scripture, to forgive someone who has wronged us, or to go and seek forgiveness from someone we've wronged. But the main point of Bible study is to apply the Truth of God's Word to your own heart.[2]

SEEKING ANSWERS FROM GOD'S WORD

- Psalm 119
- John 1:1
- John 14:26

Question 4

My prayer life feels weak. How can I pray more effectively?

A: Have you ever listened to someone else pray and thought, "I wish I could pray like her!"? Have you experienced the effects of others praying for you and wondered, "How can I pray more effectively for others?" Or perhaps you are new to prayer and you are wondering, "How is a Christian supposed to pray, in general? Is there a certain approach I'm supposed to take or certain things that should show up in my prayers?"

Consider Luke 11. This chapter records that the disciples had questions about prayer, too.

> Now Jesus was praying in a certain place, and when he finished, one of his disciples said to him, "Lord, teach us to pray, as John taught his disciples." (v. 1)

These were the men who had sacrificed their comfort to follow Jesus. They had heard Him teach. They had seen Him heal. And yet they wondered aloud about how to pray. Even fully devoted followers of Christ, like the disciples, need the Lord's help to develop a rich, effective prayer life.

Jesus responded with a short, powerful prayer.

And he said to them, "When you pray, say:

'Father, hallowed be your name.

Your kingdom come.

Give us each day our daily bread,

and forgive us our sins,

> for we ourselves forgive everyone who is indebted to us.

And lead us not into temptation.'" (Luke 11:2–4)

The Lord's Prayer provided a model. Similarly, it is helpful to have models and strategies to lean on when your prayer life feels weak. Here are some practical suggestions:

- **Pray with an eternal perspective in mind.** Ask God to use this particular situation in your life for the advancement of His kingdom. Don't always ask God to "fix" or "heal" or "provide abundantly." Sometimes "abundance" hinders you or the individual you are praying for from being more conformed to His image (2 Cor. 4:17–18).

- **When someone asks for prayer, if at all possible pray together right then.**

- **Ask the Holy Spirit to bring this request to mind** and to help you remember to keep praying.

- **Write down the prayer request.**

- **When someone you know is facing a severe trial, ask if you can include a group of Christ-followers for a specific time of prayer over him or her.** Enlist others to pray at specific times in order to have a regular cycle of intercession.

- **Seize the moment.** When you're driving and you spot a familiar car in traffic, when you pass a friend's house, or when hearing a song that reminds you of someone—pray for that person.

- **Keep reports or updates from ministries** in order to pray for specific needs.

- **Deal with distractions.** If your prayer time is interrupted by thoughts of tasks to be done, jot them down and return to prayer.

PRAY GOD'S WORD BACK TO HIM

When you struggle to find the words to pray, consider praying God's Word right back to Him by reading Scripture as a prayer. We tend to pray for what we want. Praying Scripture helps align our desires with what God has already expressed that He wants for our lives, giving us a deeper, more meaningful prayer life.

Here is a selection of verses to pray by topic:

- When you are afraid.
  - Psalm 18:1–3
  - Psalm 56
  - 1 Peter 5:7

- When you want to praise God.
  - Psalm 34:1–4
  - Psalm 59:16–17
  - Habakkuk 3:17–19

- When you are tempted to sin.
  - Psalm 119:11
  - Ephesians 6:10–11
  - James 4:7

- When you need wisdom.
  - Proverbs 2:1–6
  - James 1:5–8
  - Philippians 4:6

BUILDING A PRAYER JOURNAL

You can come to God anytime, anyplace, to pray about anything. You don't have to use a prayer journal or set specific times to pray; however, a plan can help you to be diligent.

One idea is to get a large loose-leaf binder or day planner containing a monthly calendar and pages that can be easily added or removed. Give each individual and ministry you'd like to pray for its own page, and use that to record Scriptures that apply to their needs. As a record of God's faithfulness, log dates of prayer requests and answers received.

Here are some prayer sections and Scriptures you could add:

- Daily: Pray for family and close friends.
  - For your husband or friends:
    - Ephesians 1:17–19
    - Psalm 15:1–2; 92:12–15
    - Colossians 1:9–12
  - For your children or other kids on your list:
    - 2 Corinthians 13:7–9
    - 1 Timothy 4:12; 6:11–12
    - 2 Timothy 2:22
    - Proverbs 2:20
  - Sunday: Pray for your church leadership.
    - 1 Peter 5:8
    - Romans 1:11–12
    - 2 Timothy 4:2
- Monday–Saturday: Pray for various ministries, revival, your nation and its leaders, your friends, and members of your church.

- Praises: Record answered prayers. Thank God for His work in your life.

Weaknesses in your prayer life are opportunities to showcase God's power. Scripture promises, "Likewise the Spirit helps us in our weakness. For we do not know what to pray for as we ought, but the Spirit himself intercedes for us with groanings too deep for words" (Rom. 8:26).

Like the disciples, ask the Lord to help you grow in the area of prayer. Don't be discouraged if you don't see answers to your prayers right away. Don't grow weary. It is a rich reward to see prayers answered after years of faithful intercession.

SEEKING ANSWERS FROM GOD'S WORD

- Matthew 5:44
- Ephesians 6:18
- James 5:16

Question 5

Do I really need the Church?

A: Picture this: It's Sunday morning. You've got to get yourself and three little ones dressed and out the door in time for church. Just as you are heading out the door, the littlest one spills her orange juice all over her dress. After cleaning up the mess, you're running late. You pull into the parking lot after the service has already started. Rather than checking in late to childcare, you take the kids with you into the sanctuary. They wiggle through the worship songs. They whine through the sermon. They fidget through the prayer. You want to visit with friends after the service, but it's hard to juggle coats and kids in the church lobby. By the time you get home from church you need a nap—rather, everybody needs a nap! And you've already forgotten what the sermon was about.

Sound familiar?

Perhaps you're not in the stage of life where wrangling preschoolers makes church attendance feel like a herculean feat. Maybe it's chronic pain that makes getting up and going a challenge or past hurts that make going to church sting. Perhaps you've wrestled with questions like these:

- I don't get a lot out of church. Is it really necessary?

- I struggle with so many things about the Church. Do I really need it?

- Can't I have a strong relationship with Jesus without being involved in an organized church?

When you consider the Church, perhaps you picture the building where you worship each Sunday or a place where Christians gather. The Church is bigger and more important than a building. Its significance goes far beyond your weekly routines.

Scripture tells us that Jesus is the head of the Church (Eph. 5:23), which is made up of all believers from all of time, everywhere in the world. The local church is a group of Christ-followers who are organized to encourage and equip each other and to spread the gospel together.

The Bible gives the Church assignments. Though not an exhaustive list, some of those assignments include the following:

- Teaching and admonishing each other in wisdom (Col. 3:16).

- Gathering to praise and give thanks to God (Col. 3:16).

- Proclaiming what God has done (1 Pet. 2:9–10).

- Making disciples of all nations, baptizing them in the name of the Father, the Son, and the Holy Spirit (Matt. 28:19).

- Teaching God's Word (Matt. 28:20).

- Encouraging one another (1 Thess. 5:11).

- Praying for one another (James 5:14).

- Stirring Christians up toward righteousness and good deeds (Heb. 10:24).

- Proclaiming the gospel (1 Cor. 11:26).

- Caring for the needs of the lost and hurting with compassion (2 Cor. 1:3–4).

Make your own list. What are some of the responsibilities given to the Church that you see in Scripture or have experienced in your own life?

_____

_____

_____

This mission is so vital and so big that all of God's people are needed to participate. Every "part" or person is essential to the function of Christ's Body, the Church (1 Cor. 12:21–26).

Since every Christ-follower is an essential part of His Church, perhaps a better question to ask is, can the Church thrive if Christians choose not to be involved? The answer is clearly no.

LOVING CHRIST'S BRIDE

Your own feelings toward the Church are important but are secondary to what God says about the church. God's Word is clear—Jesus loves the Church.

> Christ loved the church and gave himself up for her, that he might sanctify her, having cleansed her by the washing of water with the word, so that he might present the church to himself in splendor, without spot or wrinkle or any such thing, that she might be holy and without blemish. (Eph. 5:25–27)

The final book of the Bible, Revelation, describes the moment when God's people are finally united with Him forever. The language used describes a wedding, and the Church is Christ's cherished Bride (Rev. 19:7–9). If Christ loved the Church enough to give His life for her, shouldn't we also esteem her? If the Church is the Bride of Christ, shouldn't we also treasure her?

Though Christ's Bride will ultimately be presented to Him "bright and pure" (v. 8), the Church is still full of broken people. Challenges arise in every church because we live in a fallen world and are dealing with fellow believers who are in the process of sanctification. The Lord is the only secure object for our trust. People will and do fail us, even within the Church.

Though imperfect, the Church is God's idea. He is at work to transform Christians within the Church and to use the Church to transform the world.

As Nancy DeMoss Wolgemuth says, "Christ is 'among' the churches (Rev. 1:12–13). Despite their failures, He doesn't walk away or disengage. He stays actively engaged with them and earnestly seeks to bring them to repentance and restoration. This should be the heart of every believer for their (His) church."[3]

BETTER TOGETHER

God has given us the Church as a gift. Consider the list of the Church's assignments above and how each one can enrich your walk with Christ.

- Where can you hear wise teaching? The Church! (Col. 3:16)

- Where can you gather to praise God alongside other believers? The Church! (Col. 3:16)

- Who listens when you proclaim what God has done? The Church! (1 Pet. 2:9–10)

- Where can you be equipped to fulfill the Great Commission? The Church! (Matt. 28:19)

- Where can you receive encouragement for the Christian walk? The Church! (1 Thess. 5:11)

- Who will pray for you? The Church! (James 5:14)

- Who will stir you up toward righteousness and good deeds? The Church! (Heb. 10:24)

- Who will remind you of the gospel? The Church! (1 Cor. 11:26)

- Who will help you care for the needs of the lost and hurting with compassion? You guessed it. The Church! (2 Cor. 1:3–4)

Podcasts, online sermons, articles, or a website can dispense information, but they can't replace community. The Christian life is personal, but it is not private. It is meant to be shared. You need the people at your church, and they need you.

SEEKING ANSWERS FROM GOD'S WORD

- Matthew 16:18
- Acts 2:42–47
- Hebrews 10:24–25
- 1 Corinthians 12:12–31

Question 6

If God loves me, why am I suffering?

A: These women have asked the same question:

> I went through a scary, ugly divorce that started six years ago and took over three years to finalize. I lost my mom when I was eighteen and haven't lived near family my whole adult life. —Sadie

> At age thirty-nine, I unexpectedly ended up in the hospital for forty-six days. Five surgeries, a stay in the intensive care unit, and a slow recovery created a season of intense suffering. —Laura

> Last July I had my second heart attack. It affected my spirit in a way that I never expected. I know God is sovereign over all things, but I'm struggling inside with my recent ordeal. —Sue

This is a snapshot of the trials we hear about every day at *Revive Our Hearts*. Though many popular writers and teachers have promised God's people prosperity and peace here on earth, suffering in various forms is present in most of our lives, causing many to question the goodness of God.

Because we live in a world broken by sin, challenges like the spread of viruses, economic crises, and personal hardship will continue until Christ returns to establish a new sin-free heaven and earth. God allows suffering as a result of sin, but that doesn't mean He is not at work in the midst of the trials we face.

NO BAIT AND SWITCH

God's Word never promises a suffering-free existence for those who will follow Christ. In fact, Jesus was clear: suffering will continue as long as we remain broken people on a broken planet.

> "I have said these things to you, that in me you may have peace. In the world you will have tribulation. But take heart; I have overcome the world." (John 16:33)

Jesus didn't promise peace because of the absence of trials, but in the midst of them.

> "Truly, truly, I say to you, you will weep and lament, but the world will rejoice. You will be sorrowful, but your sorrow will turn into joy." (John 16:20)

The fact is that Jesus never offered His followers a problem-free life. Our true hope is in the promise that He has redeemed us from the ultimate suffering caused by our sin, and He has made a way for us to spend eternity in heaven with Him, free from all earthly suffering.

As we struggle through trials, God's Word gives us powerful Truths to hold on to:

- **You are not alone.** You have Christ. He walks with you. He's promised to be with you always (Matt. 28:20). The presence of Christ is a gift to help you endure.

- **You are a part of God's family.** He has given you other believers to help encourage you through trials (1 Thess. 5:11).

- **All wrongs will be righted.** Those who oppose the Truth will be brought to justice. God will

handle them. Any seeming victory they may
have is only an appearance of a victory, and it
will be short-lived (Rom. 12:19).

- **The Lord will rescue you from all trouble.** You
  can be sure of that in the future. In His way and
  in His time, He will deliver you (Psalm 34:17).

- **All your efforts, labors, suffering, and
  faithfulness under fire will be rewarded on the
  day when we receive rewards for faithfulness.**
  God has promised blessings to those who
  remain steadfast under trial (James 1:12–18).

LORD, DON'T WASTE MY SUFFERING

Your perception of suffering will ultimately be shaped by your perception of the character of God. If you question the goodness or sovereignty of God, you will resist suffering. If instead you believe God's promise to work all things ultimately to your good (Rom. 8:28), you will embrace suffering as a pathway to grow in Christ and to gain greater intimacy with God.

Jesus, our Savior, suffered for us. His Word invites us to share in His sufferings as a means of displaying His love to a lost and hurting world.

> Beloved, do not be surprised at the fiery trial when
> it comes upon you to test you, as though something
> strange were happening to you. But rejoice insofar
> as you share Christ's sufferings, that you may also
> rejoice and be glad when his glory is revealed.
> (1 Pet. 4:12–13)

Ultimately, it is impossible to be holy apart from suffering. Jesus modeled this during His time on earth, "although he was a son, he learned obedience through what he suffered" (Heb. 5:8). If you desire to be like Jesus, embrace the tools He uses, even suffering, to shape you into a better reflection of His image.[4]

SEEKING ANSWERS FROM GOD'S WORD

- Psalm 27:10
- Psalm 30:5
- 1 Corinthians 4:5
- 1 Peter 5

Question 7

I'm struggling to forgive people who have wronged me. Can you help?

A: We live in a broken world. Offenses are unavoidable. You will get hurt and you will hurt others, which means you will have many opportunities to offer and seek forgiveness. Yet there are times when the pain of an offense is so deep that forgiveness feels impossible.

We've heard from countless individuals who have experienced the heartache of bitterness and unforgiveness in their homes, in their friendships, and even in their churches:

- Wives who struggle to forgive husbands.

- Husbands who struggle to forgive wives.

- Adult children who struggle to forgive their parents.

- Parents who struggle to forgive their prodigal children.

- Church members who struggle to forgive their pastor.

- Pastors who struggle to forgive their church members.

- Friends who can't seem to get over past hurts and disappointments.

- The list goes on and on ...

Unforgiveness inevitably leads to bitterness. Bitterness may be common but it can not be acceptable in the life of the Christ-follower because bitterness hinders the flow of God's abundant grace in our lives.

In Matthew 6:15, Jesus promises, "but if you do not forgive others their trespasses, neither will your Father forgive your trespasses."

How can you know if bitterness has taken hold in your heart? For starters, see if you relate to any of these statements:

- I often replay in my mind the incident(s) that hurt me.
- When I think of a particular person or situation, I still feel angry.
- I try hard not to think about the person or circumstance that caused me so much pain.
- I have a subtle, secret desire to see this person pay for what he or she did to me.
- Deep in my heart, I wouldn't mind if something bad happened to the person(s) who hurt me.
- I often find myself telling others how this person has hurt me.
- A lot of my conversations revolve around this situation.
- Whenever his or her name comes up, I am more likely to say something negative than something positive about him or her.[5]

If the questions on this list reveal pockets of resentment and bitterness, there is urgent work to be done, as Nancy points out in her book *Choosing Forgiveness*.

Most of us know from experience that when sin of any kind is given a chance to take up residence in our hearts, it doesn't stay confined to its own little corner. If not confessed and repented of, sooner or later it will affect our entire person—our physical and emotional well-being, our demeanor, our whole outlook.

And unforgiveness is no different. When we fail to deal with hurts God's way, when we harbor resentment in our hearts, that bitterness—like an infection—will fester and work its way into our system, until ultimately we start viewing everything through the eyes of hurt—everything others do, everything that happens to us.[6]

WHAT'S MY MOTIVATION?

You cannot forgive others in the power of your own strength. You desperately need the grace of God to give you the power, ability, and even desire to do what is right. Forgiveness is not a feeling; it is a choice, an act of our will. If we waited until we felt like forgiving before we forgave, we might never forgive. We are not to wait for our emotions but rather to choose to obey God.

God commands us to forgive, regardless of how we feel and regardless of what has been done to us.

> "And wherever you stand praying, forgive, if you have anything against anyone, so that your Father also who is in heaven may forgive your trespasses." (Mark 11:25)

Scripture also reminds us that forgiveness is not in response to perceived human justice. We don't forgive because the person who hurt us has repented, because they deserve forgiveness, or because we are confident they can never hurt us again. **We forgive because God has forgiven us.**

> Be kind to one another, tenderhearted, forgiving one another, as God in Christ forgave you. (Eph. 4:32)

God's forgiveness is so radical, He willingly sent His Son, Jesus, to sacrifice His life so that you could experience forgiveness. Psalm 103:12 says "as far as the east is from the west, so far does he remove our transgressions from us." God does not deal with us as our sins deserve; rather, He forgives us and offers us mercy and kindness. God's mercy is infinite, unconditional, complete, and undeserved. He calls His children to respond to each other in the same way.

Forgiveness is pressing the delete key. It is clearing the record of the one who has sinned against us. That doesn't mean the person never sinned. It just means you're clearing the record so he or she no longer owes you for those sins. You're promising never to hold it against that person again. The results of responding as God calls you to are miraculous.[7]

Nancy writes,

> I have seen God do the unbelievable as His children have been willing not only to forgive their offenders, but to step out and return good for evil ... I often counsel women, "Believe it or not, if you'll let Him, God can actually fill your heart with deep love and compassion for that person you have hated for years!" And I have seen Him do just that.
>
> Yes, it is a miracle of God's grace. It is a miracle you can experience—not just once, but over and over again, as you cultivate a heart of forgiveness— forgiving others, as He has forgiven you.[8]

SEEKING ANSWERS FROM GOD'S WORD

- Matthew 6:14
- Luke 6:37
- Mark 11:25
- Colossians 3:13

Question 8

I'm confused about the gender debate. What does the Bible say?

A: *Revive Our Hearts* receives many emails from women who entered marriage with vivid dreams of a meaningful relationship and instead live in a world of tension, hurt, and frustration. Their romantic dreams have turned into unfulfilled expectations, bitterness toward men, and disillusionment about marriage.

One listener wrote,

> I am at the end of myself. My husband has fallen asleep in front of the TV for three years and I am downright bitter and hateful, because he doesn't love me or hold me as a husband should. I am feeling weary and hateful, which I know is wrong: I slam doors and pout but cannot tell him why I am so angry. Now he says he is tired of being mistreated. All he has done for years is yell and scream and scare me. So, I am the bad guy? I await God's answer to these prayer requests, but in the meantime I am angry and tired.

Another shared,

> From the very beginning of our marriage, my husband's only desire has been the fulfillment of his sexual "needs." Sex is an idol to him. He was very demanding and would get angry when it didn't

happen. I got pregnant right away with our first child and he was angry about that ... If he would have only loved me, loved me like he loves himself, was kind to me, he would have the wife and sex that he wanted. As it is now, I want nothing to do with him. I don't know where to turn. I hurt so deeply from this man that I trusted to love me and to build me up in Christ.

Men write heart-wrenching emails to our ministry, too.

"I am a really frustrated husband," one man wrote.

[My wife] says she believes in the scriptural view of marriage; however, she is constantly arguing with me and telling me that I am wrong about everything. (I know "everything" sounds like an exaggeration, but forty to fifty times a day sure seems like everything.) If I get up the nerve to do a chore or two around the house, she stops dead in her tracks and very critically observes me to make sure I am doing everything correctly.

These emails represent a widespread struggle to understand God's design for manhood and womanhood and to see that design lived out in the context of holy marriages.

GENDER: THE BOOKENDS OF THE BIBLE

The very first chapter of the Bible describes the creation of man and women as distinct.

> So God created man in his own image,
> in the image of God he created him;
> *male and female* he created them. (Gen. 1:27, emphasis added)

Just a few verses later, Scripture records the first wedding as Adam and Eve become "one flesh" (Gen. 2:24–25).

The final verses of God's Word also describe a wedding.
"Hallelujah!
For the Lord our God
   the Almighty reigns.
Let us rejoice and exult
   and give him the glory,
for the marriage of the Lamb has come,
   and his Bride has made herself ready."
(Rev. 19:6–7)

Scripture starts with a description of male and female, husband and wife, and it ends with a wedding. These are the bookends of Scripture, highlighting the importance of understanding and living out God's design.

While God's Word does not change, the culture certainly has. Gender is now seen as fluid. Gender confusion has reached levels we've never seen before. This is not merely a theoretical debate for the culture to spar over. Failure to understand and live out God's design for men and women has real-life implications in our homes, in our churches, and in the workplace.

CREATED DISTINCT

As Genesis 1:27 describes the creation of mankind, it points to two distinct genders, "male and female he created them." Genesis 2 provides a more detailed account of how God created the first woman, revealing that Eve was created to meet a specific need: "it is not good that the man should be alone; I will make him a helper fit for him" (v. 18).

Scripture affirms that men and women are both created in the image of God. Both genders have equal worth, value, and dignity. Men and women are invited to come to God and experience the forgiveness of sins through the blood of Jesus. Yet Scripture does not see men and women as interchangeable or gender roles as fluid. "Equality" does not mean "sameness." Men and women have distinct and vital roles to play in God's plan.

> If we're all interchangeable pieces then it's like we're just lined up and all doing the same thing like marching together. But when you begin to understand that God created male and female as complementary parts, it's like a dance with one another. There's more beauty there, and there's more unity there. There's more harmony there than is possible if you're just lined up side by side.[9] —Mary Kassian

Men and women are designed to complement each other. Our differences are meant to reveal a more complete picture of God.

> God's eternal power and His divine nature find their ultimate expression in Christ. Together, male and female (gender) testify to the character of God and portray the greatest reality of Christ and the Church. This spiritual truth is so magnificent that God chose to put it on prominent display through the entire world. He stamped the trailer for His story on every human being who has ever lived.[10]

In Ephesians 5, the apostle Paul described the unique roles and union of husband and wife before writing, "this mystery is profound, and I am saying that it refers to Christ and the church" (v. 32). Men and women being equal yet different reflects the very nature of God, and the marriage covenant between husband and wife pictures Christ's relationship with His Church. Therefore, gender cannot be insignificant. It is the imprint of His image on the world.

GOD'S GOOD PLAN

God's plan for gender is not only right and true, it is beautiful and good. God's design leads to the flourishing of mankind. The world is in rebellion against God and has veered from God's good plan for gender and marriage. The consequences are catastrophic. When we reject God's view of gender, it is always at our own peril.

> If it is true that God created gender and sexuality and male and female and created us in His image—we're created in His image, to put His glory on display—then is it any wonder that Satan is attacking us at that very point, on that very issue that displays the glory of God and that is who we are as male and female and marriage.[11] —Mary Kassian

The world may continue peddling ideas about gender that are contrary to God's Word, but by humbly acknowledging that God knows best (Isa. 55:8–9), you can gratefully receive His design for you and put His image on display to a lost and hurting world.

SEEKING ANSWERS FROM GOD'S WORD

- Genesis 1:26–27
- 1 Corinthians 8:6
- Ephesians 5:22–23
- Colossians 1:16

Question 9

What is revival? Can we really experience it?

A: Though Jenni had been a Christian for many years, her prayer life was weak. Her time in God's Word was stale. She was going through the motions of the Christian life: attending church regularly, volunteering in the nursery, going to Bible study, but the passion she once felt to hear and obey God was gone. Most days, she read her Bible and went on with her day, immediately forgetting what she'd read.

Then Jenni's husband was deployed to serve in the Middle East. During those long months alone, God began to stir Jenni's heart in new ways. Her desire to read the Bible returned. Soon she couldn't read it often enough to satisfy her craving for the Word. She drew near to God's people with renewed need. She sought the Lord with fresh passion. The results sent shockwaves through her friends and family. After his return from deployment, Jenni's husband decided to be baptized. So did her two children. Her friends started gathering regularly to read the Bible together and pray. Her church was revitalized. Jenni experienced true revival.

Depending on your background, the word *revival* may carry some baggage or sound like an old-fashioned concept. Revival is a label that has been applied to a variety of happenings, including:

- An annual series of religious meetings (with activities ranging from meaningful and helpful to bizarre and unbiblical).

- Evangelism campaigns designed to reach out to the lost.

- Seasons of widespread, increased religious fervor.

- Moral and social change.

While some of the things on this list may be present during revival, they don't get to the heart of true revival.

WHAT COMES TO MIND WHEN YOU THINK OF REVIVAL? WRITE DOWN A FEW NOTES BELOW.

_____

_____

_____

Revival is not an event we can schedule on the calendar. Nor is it synonymous with *evangelism*, though when revival comes, unbelievers will surrender their lives to Jesus. Revival often stirs our emotions, but true revival is deeper than excitement and enthusiasm.

So, what is revival, really? How can we know if it is genuine?

REVIVAL = LIFE AGAIN

The word revive literally means "to bring back to life." Another way to say it is "life again." Revival happens when God's people are restored to a right relationship with Him.

REVIVAL IS FOR THE CHURCH

Those who are still dead in their sins cannot experience life again. It is God's people, God's Church, that needs to be revived.

Revival is a supernatural work of God—it is not something we can manufacture or package. In times of personal or corporate revival, God's people experience His presence and power in ways previously missing from their lives and to degrees they may not have thought possible. A revived church is the greatest means of making God's redemptive plan known throughout the world.

How can we become a revived Church? How can we experience the kind of revival that Jenni did?

In the early 1900s the Spirit of God began to stir in an extraordinary way in the hearts of believers throughout the Principality of Wales. What transpired over the next several months was nothing short of supernatural.

"Bend the Church, and save the world!" was the cry that rang out through villages and towns, in the churches, and in the hearts of men, women, and children, and young people throughout all of Wales.

Evan Roberts was one human instrument that God used in this season. The fire of God burned in the heart of this twenty-six-year-old coal miner who had little formal education. Everywhere he went, Evan Roberts delivered a message that was simple, straightforward, and timeless. It became known as "The Four Points." Did God's people desire an outpouring of His Spirit? Then four conditions must be observed:

- Confess all known sin.
- Put away all doubtful things and forgive everyone.
- Obey the prompting of the Holy Spirit.
- Publicly confess Christ as your Savior.

"DO IT AGAIN, LORD!"

Few people today have ever witnessed revival and spiritual awakening on a scale as magnificent as the Welsh revival (though God is doing a remarkable work in certain pockets of the world). There is a growing sense of longing and desperation among believers to see God "do it again!"

The God who displayed His glory in the great awakenings of the past is the same God we worship today. He has not changed. He is no less able to turn the heart of a nation today than He was 100 years ago! He is willing—yes, eager—to manifest Himself and His saving grace to the lost, prodigal planet. But first, we must have a revived church. And a revived church consists of revived individuals. So, how does revival start? Historically, when a community or nation has experienced awakening and revival, it has always been preceded by intense periods of prayer.

Revival is the work of a Sovereign God, but Scripture indicates He listens and responds when His people cry out in humility and repentance. Here are some key things to keep in mind as you pray for revival:

- Confess corporate sin.
- Humble yourself before God, and depend on His power.
- Make requests on the basis of God's character (He is faithful; He keeps His promises; He is compassionate; etc.).
- Desire that God's reputation and name be vindicated and for His glory to be seen.

The Psalmist said, "You who seek God, let your hearts revive" (Psalm 69:32). If you will seek Him with all your heart, you can be confident that He will restore, renew, and revive you. That revival will soon affect others.

God does not lavish His goodness on us so we can simply enjoy it for ourselves. We have been saved to "proclaim the excellencies of him who called [us] out of darkness into his marvelous light" (1 Pet. 2:9). One person, one family, one small group, one church—no matter how "insignificant"—that is committed to seeking the Lord can become a tool God uses to revive others and to spread His glory throughout the world.[12]

Note: This answer is adapted from *Seeking Him: Experiencing the Joy of Personal Revival* by Nancy DeMoss Wolgemuth and Tim Grissom (Moody). Used by permission.

SEEKING ANSWERS FROM GOD'S WORD

- 2 Chronicles 7:14
- Psalm 80:19
- Psalm 85:6

Question 10

Can Christians really make a difference?

A: Terrorism.

Child abuse.

Cancer.

Domestic violence.

War.

Genocide.

The list of evils plaguing this world is long. Satan is truly the "prince of the power of the air" and he is at work to cause death and destruction across the world God created (John 10:10).

As the darkness presses in around us, it can be tempting to throw up our hands in defeat or to drift toward disillusionment that God's people can really make a dent in the problems of this world. What does God's Word say?

ULTIMATE HOPE

There is no power, no nation, no force, no institution, no human system, no ruler, and no person that is so great that God cannot bring it down in a moment if and when He chooses. He has promised that the darkness will not prevail.

> Then I saw a new heaven and a new earth, for the first heaven and the first earth had passed away, and the sea was no more. And I saw the holy city, new

Jerusalem, coming down out of heaven from God, prepared as a bride adorned for her husband. And I heard a loud voice from the throne saying, "Behold, the dwelling place of God is with man. He will dwell with them, and they will be his people, and God himself will be with them as their God. He will wipe away every tear from their eyes, and death shall be no more, neither shall there be mourning, nor crying, nor pain anymore, for the former things have passed away." (Rev. 21:1–4)

AMBASSADORS OF LIGHT

As He ascended to the Father following His resurrection, Jesus called all Christians to push back against the darkness.

"All authority in heaven and on earth has been given to me. Go therefore and make disciples of all nations, baptizing them in the name of the father and of the Son and of the Holy Spirit, teaching them to observe all that I have commanded you." (Matt. 28:18–20)

Jesus wasn't giving us busy work with no intended results. Instead, He has unleashed the Church to join Him in the mission of reaching the lost and teaching His Word.

God has not forsaken the world He created. He's not oblivious to the injustices and heartaches so many are experiencing. He has sent out His Church as ambassadors for Truth in a world in desperate need of it.

While we await the new heaven and new earth, Christians have been given clear assignments:

- **Live as children of the light** (Eph. 5:8).

- **Resist hate by loving one another** (John 13:34–35).

- **Share the gospel** (Mark 16:15).

- **Make disciples** (Matt. 28:19).

- **Teach the Word** (Matt. 28:20).

- **Comfort the hurting** (2 Cor. 1:3).

- **Give to the poor** (Prov. 19:17).

We are called to live set apart lives.

"You are the salt of the earth, but if salt has lost its taste, how shall its saltiness be restored? It is no longer good for anything except to be thrown out and trampled under people's feet."

"You are the light of the world. A city set on a hill cannot be hidden. Nor do people light a lamp and put it under a basket, but on a stand, and it gives light to all in the house. In the same way, let your light shine before others, so that they may see your good works and give glory to your Father who is in heaven." (Matt. 5:13–16)

What difference can living for Jesus possibly make? Ask Graciela.

Graciela is one of six thousand women who attended *Revive Our Hearts'* Mujer Verdadera conference in Mexico in early 2020. She was not a follower of Jesus but had been invited to attend by some Christian women in her community.

That conference ended just as the coronavirus began to spread around the globe, preventing Graciela from returning home for several weeks. Christians in Mexico took Graciela in and discipled her daily. The world was shutting down, but Graciela's heart was opening up. She surrendered her life to Jesus. Upon her return to Colombia, Christians in her community surrounded Graciela and continued to teach her what it means to live like Christ.

Within a few months, Graciela contracted the coronavirus. The virus eventually took her life. But Graciela was a changed woman. She spent her final days testifying to God's work in her life and praying for her family and friends who did not know Jesus.

What difference can Christians make? In Graciela's case, the difference was eternal. It was God who changed her heart, but He used the words, invitations, and examples of Christians to draw her to Him.

Consider your own faith.

- What difference did the example of Christians make as you were coming to faith?

- How have Christians encouraged you during challenging times?

- How have Christians equipped you to live out your faith in Christ?

- How have you seen the Church make a difference in your community?

The Church is making a difference. Darkness and evil will continue to spread until Christ's return, but we have been given the awesome responsibility to be bearers of hope.

SEEKING ANSWERS FROM GOD'S WORD

- Lamentations 3:21–23

- Isaiah 65:17–19

- 2 Peter 3:10–13

Small Group Guide

Q1. I THINK I'M A CHRISTIAN, BUT I'M NOT SURE. HOW CAN I BE CERTAIN?

ADDITIONAL SCRIPTURE:

- Jude 24–25
- 1 Peter 1:3–5
- Philippians 1:6

RECOMMENDED RESOURCES:

- *How Can I Be Sure I'm a Christian?* by Donald S. Whitney
- "Do You Know Him?" article by Blair Linne. Find it at ReviveOurHearts.com.
- *Transforming Grace: Living Confidently in God's Unfailing Love* by Jerry Bridges
- *Rahab: Tracing the Thread of Redemption*, Women of the Bible Study from *Revive Our Hearts*.

DISCUSSION QUESTIONS:

- How would you describe grace?
- What difference does your confidence in Christ make in your daily life?
- What are some ways you can remind yourself of the promises of God when questions or doubts arise?

Q2. HOW COULD GOD POSSIBLY FORGIVE WHAT I'VE DONE?

ADDITIONAL SCRIPTURE:

- Romans 5:8–10
- 2 Peter 3:9
- Psalm 103:10–12
- 1 John 2:1–2

RECOMMENDED RESOURCES:

- *Lies Women Believe and the Truth That Sets Them Free* by Nancy DeMoss Wolgemuth
- *Brokenness: The Heart God Revives* by Nancy DeMoss Wolgemuth
- *Jesus Keep Me Near the Cross* by Nancy Guthrie

DISCUSSION QUESTIONS:

- How can you experience true freedom from the weight of your sin?
- Are there any sins you need to repent of and bring into the light?
- How can you encourage someone who is struggling to believe God's grace?

Q3. I GET SO DISTRACTED WHEN I TRY TO READ THE BIBLE. HOW CAN I FOCUS?

ADDITIONAL SCRIPTURE:

- Joshua 1:8
- 1 Timothy 4:13
- Psalm 1:2–3
- Psalm 119:105

RECOMMENDED RESOURCES:

- *A Place of Quiet Rest: Finding Intimacy with God through a Daily Devotional Life* by Nancy DeMoss Wolgemuth
- *A 30-Day Walk with God in the Psalms* by Nancy DeMoss Wolgemuth
- *Lord, Teach Me to Study the Bible in 28 Days* by Kay Arthur
- *How to Study Your Bible* by Kay Arthur
- *His Word in My Heart: Memorizing Scripture for a Closer Walk with God* by Janet Pope
- "Reviving a Lifeless Bible Study" article by Laura Booz. Find it at ReviveOurHearts.com.

DISCUSSION QUESTIONS:

- What are the benefits of studying God's Word?
- What are some practical ways to start studying your Bible?

- What topic of spiritual growth would you like to explore?

- Who in your life can help keep you accountable to daily study of God's Word?

Q4. MY PRAYER LIFE FEELS WEAK. HOW CAN I PRAY MORE EFFECTIVELY?

ADDITIONAL SCRIPTURE:

- Matthew 6:5–6
- Luke 18:1–8
- Philippians 4:6
- 1 John 5:14–15

RECOMMENDED RESOURCES:

- *Praying the Bible* by Donald S. Whitney
- *My Personal Petitions Prayer Journal* by Nancy DeMoss Wolgemuth
- *The Battle Plan for Prayer* by Stephen Kendrick and Alex Kendrick with Travis Agnew
- "Seven Kinds of Prayer to Soak Our Bible Reading" article by John Piper. Find it at ReviveOurHearts.com.

DISCUSSION QUESTIONS

- How can you know God better through prayer?
- What are some ways you can incorporate prayer into your everyday life?
- What is one practical step you can take to invigorate your prayer life?

Q5. DO I REALLY NEED THE CHURCH?

ADDITIONAL SCRIPTURE:

- Romans 12:4–5
- 1 Corinthians 14:26
- Ephesians 5:19

RECOMMENDED RESOURCES:

- *Adorned: Living Out the Beauty of the Gospel Together* by Nancy DeMoss Wolgemuth
- *What Is a Healthy Church?* by Mark Dever
- *Word-Filled Women's Ministry* by Gloria Furman and Kathleen B. Nielson

DISCUSSION QUESTIONS:

- How does the Church impact your walk with Christ?
- Are you struggling to have a good attitude toward the Church? Ask the Lord to change your perspective and give you a love like His for the Church.
- How might the Lord be calling you to serve within your local church?

Q6. IF GOD LOVES ME, WHY AM I SUFFERING?

ADDITIONAL SCRIPTURE:

- Romans 5:3–5
- Romans 8:18, 28
- James 1:2–4

RECOMMENDED RESOURCES:

- *Suffering Is Never for Nothing* by Elisabeth Elliot
- *Hope When It Hurts* by Kristen Wetherell and Sarah Walton
- *You Can Trust God to Write Your Story* by Nancy DeMoss Wolgemuth and Robert Wolgemuth
- *Habakkuk: Remembering God's Faithfulness When He Seems Silent* by Dannah Gresh
- *Ruth: Experiencing a Life Restored*, Women of the Bible study from *Revive Our Hearts*.

DISCUSSION QUESTIONS:

- How do you typically respond when intense trials come?
- When you are discouraged by life's challenges, what are some promises of God you can hold onto?
- How might God be using the trials in your life for something good?
- How do you see the Lord's faithfulness in the midst of our broken world?

Q7. I'M STRUGGLING TO FORGIVE PEOPLE WHO HAVE WRONGED ME. CAN YOU HELP?

ADDITIONAL SCRIPTURE:

- Hebrews 12:15
- Ephesians 2:12–16
- Romans 12:18

RECOMMENDED RESOURCES:

- *Choosing Forgiveness: Your Journey to Freedom* by Nancy DeMoss Wolgemuth
- *Freedom through Forgiveness* by Nancy DeMoss Wolgemuth
- *The Complicated Heart: Loving Even When It Hurts* by Sarah Mae
- *Forgiveness: Breaking the Power of the Past* by Kay Arthur and David & BJ Lawson
- "Forgiven, Forgiving, and Free!" article by Nancy DeMoss Wolgemuth. Find it at ReviveOurHearts.com.

DISCUSSION QUESTIONS:

- Why is it important to forgive others?
- Consider how God has forgiven you. How does this enable you to forgive those who have hurt you?
- Is there someone you need to forgive?
- Do you need to ask for forgiveness from anyone?

Q8. I'M CONFUSED ABOUT THE GENDER DEBATE. WHAT DOES THE BIBLE SAY?

ADDITIONAL SCRIPTURE:

- Titus 2:3–5
- Proverbs 14:1
- Proverbs 31:10–31
- 1 Peter 3:1–7

RECOMMENDED RESOURCES:

- *Lies Women Believe and the Truth That Sets Them Free* by Nancy DeMoss Wolgemuth
- *True Woman 101: Divine Design* by Mary Kassian and Nancy DeMoss Wolgemuth
- *True Woman 201: Interior Design* by Mary Kassian and Nancy DeMoss Wolgemuth
- *Girls Gone Wise in a World Gone Wild* by Mary Kassian
- *The Right Kind of Strong* by Mary Kassian
- *A 30-Day Journey through the True Woman Manifesto*
- "Men and Women: Similarities and Differences" article by Wayne Grudem. Find it at ReviveOurHearts.com.

DISCUSSION QUESTIONS

- In what ways does the world's definition of womanhood differ from the Bible's definition?

- What lies have you believed about how God created men and women?

- What qualities do you admire in godly women? What qualities do you hope people will notice in you?

- How does your calling as a woman shape the purpose God has given you?

Q9. WHAT IS REVIVAL? CAN WE REALLY EXPERIENCE IT?

ADDITIONAL SCRIPTURE:

- Psalm 139:23–24
- 2 Corinthians 5:17
- Jeremiah 29:13
- Psalm 67:1–2

RECOMMENDED RESOURCES:

- *Seeking Him: Experiencing the Joy of Personal Revival* by Nancy DeMoss Wolgemuth and Tim Grissom
- "Choosing Brokenness" article by Nancy DeMoss Wolgemuth. Find it at ReviveOurHearts.com
- *Revival* by Richard Owen Roberts
- *Ablaze with His Glory: A Plea for Revival in Our Time* by Del Fehsenfeld Jr.
- *Refresh: 30 Days of Personal Revival Journaling Set*

DISCUSSION QUESTIONS:

- How does revival begin?
- What are some results of revival among God's people?
- Why does God want to revive us?
- Has there been a time in your life when you have walked more closely with God than you are now? What differences have you noticed in your intimacy with Him?
- What particular area(s) of your own life do you long to see revived?

Q10. CAN CHRISTIANS REALLY MAKE A DIFFERENCE?

ADDITIONAL SCRIPTURE:

- Colossians 4:2–6
- John 1:4–5
- Philippians 2:15
- 1 John 1:5–7

RECOMMENDED RESOURCES:

- "Building Up One Another" article by Nancy DeMoss Wolgemuth. Find it at ReviveOurHearts.com.

- "Encouraging One Another" article by Nancy DeMoss Wolgemuth. Find it at ReviveOurHearts.com.

- *The Set-Apart Woman: God's Invitation to Sacred Living* by Leslie Ludy

- *Mere Christianity* by C. S. Lewis

- *Gospel Fluency: Speaking the Truths of Jesus into the Everyday Stuff of Life* by Jeff Vanderstelt

DISCUSSION QUESTIONS:

- What is an example of "living in the light"?

- How can you encourage someone with the hope of Christ?

- What are some practical ways you can demonstrate God's love to others?

- What is one Scripture passage you can memorize as a reminder to push back against the darkness?

Notes

1. Nancy DeMoss Wolgemuth, "Purity and Direction," *Revive Our Hearts*, January 5, 2009, https://www.reviveourhearts.com/podcast/revive-our-hearts/purity-and-direction-1/.

2. Nancy DeMoss Wolgemuth, "A-E-I-O-U Bible Study Method," *Revive Our Hearts*, accessed January 18, 2021, https://www.reviveourhearts.com/articles/a-e-i-o-u-bible-study-method/.

3. Nancy DeMoss Wolgemuth, text message to author.

4. Content for this answer adapted from Nancy DeMoss Wolgemuth, *Lies Women Believe: and the Truth That Sets Them Free* (Chicago, IL: Moody Publishers, 2018). Used by permission.

5. Nancy Leigh DeMoss, *Choosing Forgiveness: Your Journey to Freedom* (Chicago, IL: Moody Publishers, 2010), 58.

6. DeMoss, *Choosing Forgiveness*, 59.

7. Nancy DeMoss Wolgemuth, "Forgiven, Forgiving, and Free!," *Revive Our Hearts*, accessed January 18, 2021, https://www.reviveourhearts.com/articles/forgiven-forgiving-and-free/.

8. DeMoss, *Choosing Forgiveness*, 206.

9. Mary Kassian, "The Beauty of God's Design," *Revive Our Hearts*, December 5, 2012, https://www.reviveourhearts.com/podcast/revive-our-hearts/beauty-gods-design/.